SACRED TEXTS

The
Torah
and Judaism

Vivienne Cato

A+
Smart Apple Media

Evans Brothers Limited, 2A Portman Mansions
Chiltern St., London W1U 6NR

First published 2003
Text copyright © Evans Brothers Ltd 2003
© in the illustrations Evans Brothers Ltd 2003

Printed in Hong Kong by
Wing King Tong Co. Ltd

Editors: Nicola Barber, Louise John
Designer: Simon Borrough
Illustrations: Tracy Fennell, Allied Artists
Production: Jenny Mulvanny
Consultant: Jonathan Gorsky

Picture acknowledgements:
theartarchive: p10 (Galleria d'Arte Moderna
Venice/Dagli Orti. Hayez Francesco: 1791-
1882).
The Bridgeman Art Library: p18 (Marc
Chagall 1887-1985).
Circa Photo Library: p7
bottom/14/15/16/20/21/23/25 (Barrie
Searle), p27 (Zbigniew Kosc).
Trip: p7 top (S Shapiro), p8/9/11/13/19
(I Genut), p12 (H Rogers. Painting by Henry
Coller), p17 (J Soester), p22 (H Rogers),
p24 (S Shapiro).

Published in the United States by
Smart Apple Media, 1980 Lookout Drive
North Mankato, Minnesota 56003

Library of Congress Cataloging-in-Publication
Data

Cato, Vivienne.
The Torah and Judaism / by Vivienne Cato.
p. cm. — (Sacred texts)
Contents: Introduction — Origins —Structure
and contents — Message and teachings — Daily
life and worship — Study and reading.
ISBN 1-58340-244-6
1. Judaism—Juvenile literature. [1. Judaism. 2.
Jewish law.] I. Title: Torah and Judaism. II. Title.
III. Sacred texts (Mankato, Minn.)

BM573.C35 2003
222'.1—dc21   2003041644

First Edition
9 8 7 6 5 4 3 2 1

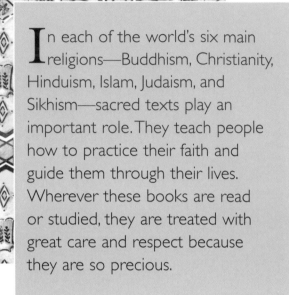

In each of the world's six main religions—Buddhism, Christianity, Hinduism, Islam, Judaism, and Sikhism—sacred texts play an important role. They teach people how to practice their faith and guide them through their lives. Wherever these books are read or studied, they are treated with great care and respect because they are so precious.

In this book, dates are written using B.C.E., which means "before the common era," and C.E., which means "of the common era." These abbreviations replace B.C. ("before Christ") and A.D. (*anno domini*, "in the year of the Lord"), which are based on the Christian calendar.

The quotations in this book come from a translation of the Hebrew Bible (The Tenakh) published by the Jewish Publication Society, 1985.

Contents

The Torah

The Torah is the sacred text of the Jewish people, who follow the religion of Judaism. In the Torah, the Jews are called "the Hebrews" and "the children of Israel," but in modern times they are known only as Jews. The word "Jew" comes from the name "Judah." Judah was one of Abraham's great-grandsons and the leader of one of the 12 Hebrew tribes. Jews believe in one God, who is everywhere. Throughout their lives, Jews try to help God make the world a better place.

How Judaism began

Judaism began about 3,800 years ago in Babylonia, which is now part of Iraq. The first Jew was Abraham. He was the first person to understand that there was only one God. Many people at this time, including Abraham's family, believed that there were many different gods. God asked Abraham to leave his family and his country. He made a covenant (agreement) with Abraham that he would become the father of a great nation. The people of this nation would be given the land of Canaan (the country that is Israel today) to live in. Canaan was known as the Promised Land. The Hebrews' special task was to spread moral teachings and to help others to understand that God was the ruler of the world.

"The Lord said to Abram*, 'Go forth from your native land and from your father's house to the land that I will show you. I will make of you a great nation, and I will bless you; I will make your name great, and you shall be a blessing.'"

(GENESIS 12: 1-2)

*ABRAHAM WAS KNOWN AS ABRAM BEFORE GOD CHANGED HIS NAME.

Judaism today

Today there are about 13 million Jews throughout the world. This is much smaller than the number of Christians, Muslims, Hindus, or Buddhists, and about the same as the number of Sikhs. Jews come from many places—including Europe, the United States, Israel, and parts of Africa. In Great Britain, there are about 300,000 Jews. However, the country with the largest number of Jews, more than five million, is the United States. There are also nearly five million Jews living in Israel. Israeli Jews speak Hebrew, the language of the Torah. Until the 20th century, Hebrew had not been spoken for 2,000 years. Elsewhere, Jews speak the language of the country in which they live, but wherever they live, Jews feel that they are members of a worldwide family.

Many Jews move from their countries to Israel, which is still considered to be the Promised Land. This mother and child are arriving in Israel from Ethiopia.

Being Jewish

A person is Jewish if his or her mother is Jewish. This is true even if he or she is not brought up as a Jew and knows nothing about the religion. People who are not born Jewish can convert later, although Judaism does not look for converts.

Israel's deserts look the same today as they did in the time of Abraham.

Origins

The Torah is given on Mount Sinai

Traditional Jews believe that God told Moses the whole of the Torah on Mount Sinai. Moses then wrote down all of God's words exactly. Less traditional Jews think that prophets and other people who were inspired by God wrote the Torah. However, nearly all Jews believe that God gave Moses the Ten Commandments. The Ten Commandments sum up some of Judaism's key points. They tell Jews how to behave toward God and toward other people.

The Ten Commandments

1. I am the Lord your God.
2. You shall have no other gods but Me. You shall not make any statues or images of anything on earth. You shall not worship them.
3. You shall not swear falsely by the name of the Lord your God.
4. Remember the Sabbath day and keep it holy.
5. Honor your father and your mother.
6. You shall not murder.
7. You shall not commit adultery.
8. You shall not steal.
9. You shall not wrongly accuse anyone.
10. You shall not covet anything that belongs to someone else.

"Moses came and summoned the elders of the people and put before them all that the Lord had commanded him. All the people answered as one, saying, 'All that the Lord has spoken we will do!' And Moses brought back the people's words to the Lord."

(EXODUS 19: 7–8)

Escape from Egypt

About 3,500 years ago, the children of Israel were slaves in Egypt, working for the pharaohs (kings). God remembered His promise to Abraham and sent Moses to lead the Israelites to freedom. Moses asked the Pharaoh to let the Israelites go, but he refused. Only after God had sent 10 horrible plagues to Egypt did the Pharaoh change his mind. Some of these plagues turned the rivers to blood, gave the Egyptians lice, and finally killed all their eldest children. Led by Moses, the Israelites escaped to the desert. Seven weeks later, God spoke to Moses on Mount Sinai. This is one of the most important moments in Jewish history.

Moses brings the Ten Commandments down from Mount Sinai.

Wandering in the desert

After escaping from Egypt, the children of Israel had to wander through the desert for 40 years before God allowed them to enter Canaan, their Promised Land. For all this time, they carried with them the two tablets of stone on which God had written the Ten Commandments. The tablets were kept in a box called the ark of the covenant. When the Jews finally built the first Temple in Jerusalem, the ark was kept in a room at its very center. This room was called the holy of holies, and only the high priest was allowed inside. The tablets and the ark of the covenant were lost after the first Temple in Jerusalem was destroyed (see page 10). Even today, no one knows where they are.

Today, every synagogue (Jewish house of prayer) has its own ark. The Ten Commandments are written in Hebrew above this one.

The history of the Jews

Moses is known among Jews as Moshe Rabbenu, "Moses Our Teacher." He is the one who met God directly and encouraged the people to keep God's commandments. Abraham is known as the first Jew, but it was receiving the Torah that made the children of Israel into one people who could be called Jewish. Since then, the Jewish people have lived through some difficult times.

The Jews are sent away

The Babylonians destroyed the first Temple in Jerusalem in 586 B.C.E. It was rebuilt, but this second Temple was also destroyed almost 500 years later, this time by the Romans. The Jewish people scattered all over the world. They were often treated badly by their neighbors because the Christian Church told its members that the Jews had killed Jesus. Many countries, including England, cast out their Jews. In countries where they were allowed to live, Jewish people were forbidden to do almost all kinds of work. But by 1800, Jews were able to live almost anywhere. Governments in Western Europe gave them the right to vote, and to make the same choices about their lives as everyone else.

Even 2,000 years later, Jews still remember the destruction of the first Temple in Jerusalem. One day each year is set aside for mourning its destruction. Adults fast, and prayers are said in a darkened synagogue.

The destruction of the second Temple in Jerusalem by the Romans.

Jewish families being rounded up by the Nazis during the Holocaust.

The Holocaust

The worst period in Jewish history took place during World War II. In Germany, Adolf Hitler and his Nazi Party spread lies that the Jews were responsible for the country's problems. Jews were imprisoned in camps, made to work as slaves, and killed in huge numbers. By the end of the war, in 1945, the Nazis had murdered six million Jews, including one and a half million children, from all over Europe. This disaster is known as the Holocaust or, in Hebrew, the Shoah.

"I have come down to rescue them from the Egyptians and to bring them out of that land to a good and spacious land, a land flowing with milk and honey."

(EXODUS 3: 8)

The State of Israel

Jews have always hoped that in the end they would be able to return to the land of Israel. In the Torah, God promised this land to Abraham and his children forever. After the Holocaust, the idea of giving it to the Jews as a home became more popular. In 1948, the State of Israel was born. Many Jews from Europe, the United States, and the Arab countries went to live there. Israel is the only Jewish State in the world, although it also contains many Muslim and Christian Arab Israelis.

Structure and Contents

The contents of the Torah

The word "Torah" actually means "teaching." The Torah is made up of five books, which are also called the Five Books of Moses. There are other books that Jews also consider to be sacred, called the Prophets and the Writings. Together they are known as the Tenakh. All of these books are also sacred for Christians, who call them the Old Testament. When Jews talk of the Torah, they sometimes mean all of these books put together. But usually, the Torah means the Five Books on their own. They are Genesis, Exodus, Leviticus, Numbers, and Deuteronomy.

What's in the Torah?

The Torah is a mixture of stories and teachings. One famous story is about how God created the first human beings, Adam and Eve, and put them in the beautiful Garden of Eden. When they disobeyed God by eating fruit from the tree of good and evil, He threw them out of the Garden. From then on, they had to work hard for their living. Another story tells of how God nearly destroyed the world with a huge flood. He felt so disappointed by humans that He saved only Noah and his family, who built a big boat, called an ark. Noah took one pair of each kind of animal with him. In this way all of creation was saved.

The animals enter Noah's ark in pairs.

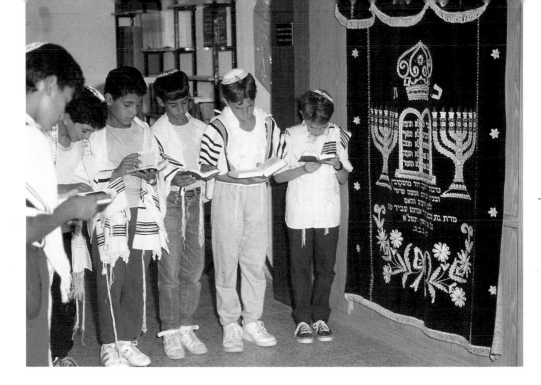

Following the commandments in the Torah, young Jewish boys say their daily prayers near the ark in a synagogue.

Book of rules

The Torah contains many rules and instructions about how Jews should live. The Ten Commandments are best known, but altogether there are 613 of these commandments. They are not written as a list, but are scattered throughout the Torah. They include the commandments not to kill or steal, and to respect one's parents. Others are about how to pray, what to eat, and which festivals to celebrate. Jews believe that they come closer to God by observing His instructions. Traditional Jews believe these commandments can never be changed. Less traditional Jews think that they can be adapted to suit modern-day life.

A famous rabbi (teacher) called Hillel lived nearly 2,000 years ago in Babylon. Someone once asked Hillel to teach him the whole Torah while standing on one leg. Hillel said, "Love your neighbor as yourself. That is the whole of the Torah. The rest is simply comment on it. Go and study." This is known as the Golden Rule.

About God

The Torah tells people what God is like. God is the Eternal Ruler, who created the world. The message of the Torah is that God cares for the Jewish people, as well as all humanity and the rest of creation. Jews believe that He still cares, and is still involved with them today.

Writing the Torah

Anyone can get a copy of the Torah in book form, but the Torah that is read aloud in synagogues is written on a scroll. It contains the whole text of the Five Books of Moses. This scroll is so long that, if unwound, it would stretch the length of a football field.

How a Torah scroll is made

A Torah scroll is made from sheets of parchment (animal skin). A specially trained person, called a sofer, writes by hand on the scroll in Hebrew. He writes with a quill made from a turkey or goose feather, and with black ink made with a special recipe. It takes him at least a year to write out the whole Torah. The sofer is not allowed to write a single word from memory. He must copy, slowly, from a book of the Torah, and keep checking for mistakes. It is important that not a single letter is smudged or touching another letter. If the sofer makes a mistake, he scrapes off the letters with a glass tool.

The most sacred word that the sofer writes is the Hebrew name for God. If he makes a mistake writing this name, he cannot correct it—he must start the whole sheet of parchment again. The sheet with the mistake on it is then buried in a Jewish cemetery.

A sofer writing a Torah.

The finished scroll

When all the sheets of parchment are finished, they are sewn together and wound around wooden rollers. The Torah is respected as holy, so it is decorated as beautifully as possible. It has a cover, called a mantle, which is usually embroidered. The tops of the rollers are dressed with silver crowns, and a silver breastplate is hung over the front of the scroll. There is also a silver pointer, called a yad, for reading with. When it is not being used, the scroll is kept in a special cupboard at the front of the synagogue, called an ark. This reminds Jews of the ark of the covenant, in which the children of Israel carried the Ten Commandments (see page 9).

"He has told you, O man, what is good, and what the Lord requires of you: only to do justice and to love goodness, and to walk modestly with your God." (MICAH 6: 8)

A new scroll

When a synagogue buys or is given a new scroll, it is a time of great celebration. Everyone joins in as the scroll is carried around the synagogue. Someone may be given the great honor of writing the last letter of the Torah to complete the scroll.

A new scroll is brought to the synagogue for the first time.

Message and Teachings

What the Torah teaches

The Torah is the source of most of the commandments or rules that guide Jews in their everyday lives. However, these rules are usually described only very briefly. The great rabbis who lived more than a thousand years ago talked a lot about what the commandments really meant. They laid down details of exactly how God's commandments were to be carried out. This set of Jewish rules to live by is known as the Halakhah, which means "the path."

Family life

For Jews, family is very important, and children learn about Judaism through everyday family life. The fifth commandment tells children to respect their parents (see page 8). When they grow up, Jewish children are expected to marry other Jews and have children of their own. Many Jewish festivals are celebrated at home and with special meals—especially Shabbat.

Shabbat—the Sabbath

Every Saturday is Shabbat, the Jewish day of rest, when Jews do no work. For traditional Jews, doing no work includes activities such as cooking, driving, or shopping. Instead, Jews go to the synagogue, study, and spend time with family and friends. This is because the Torah says that God rested

Some Jews light special candles at dusk on Friday evenings to mark the beginning of Shabbat.

on the seventh day after creating the world. On the Jewish calendar, a day runs from sunset to sunset. This means that Shabbat actually starts at dusk on Friday and ends when it gets dark on Saturday.

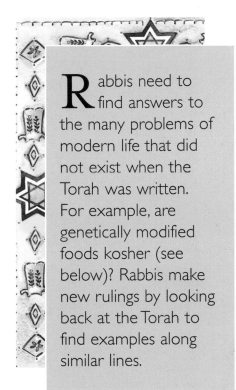

"The seventh day is a sabbath of the Lord your God; you shall not do any work—you, your son or your daughter, your male or female slave, your ox or your ass, or any of your cattle ..."

(DEUTERONOMY 5: 14)

Kosher food

The food Jews eat must be kosher, which means "ritually proper." All fruits and vegetables are allowed, but only certain kinds of meat may be eaten. Meat is kosher only from animals that have split hooves and chew cud (such as cattle), and fish that have both fins and scales. Kosher animals must be killed in a certain way so that they don't suffer much. Also, Jews cannot eat both meat and dairy foods in the same meal.

Buying bread in a Jewish bakery, where the bread is specially prepared.

Looking after other people

The Torah tells Jews that they must care for those around them. Although their families come first, Jewish people must also look after their communities and the worldwide community of Jews. They are also required to help those from other faiths or cultures. The most important value in Judaism is to protect life. This means that almost any rule can be broken to save someone's life. In general, Jews believe they are working with God to bring about Tikkun Olam—"the repair of the world."

giving money

In Judaism, giving money to charity is not something you choose to do. It is a requirement. All Jews must give 10 percent of what they earn to help others who are worse off. This is the case even if you yourself are poor. The Hebrew word for charity is "tzedaka," but it really means "doing righteous acts." This is because helping people is part of making the world a better place in which to live.

Marc Chagall painted Jewish village life in early 20th-century Russia.

Acts of kindness

Jews try to welcome friends, and especially new visitors, to their homes. They may invite someone who lives alone for a Shabbat meal. Jews also make an effort to visit the sick, comfort mourners, and give back property to any person who has lost it. All of these acts were first inspired by stories in the Torah.

Care for animals

The Torah tells Jews to be kind to animals, who, just like their owners, are not allowed to work on Shabbat. At mealtimes, farm animals or pets must be fed first. Stray animals must be returned to their owners. Hunting and any other kind of cruelty is forbidden. No animal should be killed for food in the sight of its mother or baby. This is because it would cause them distress.

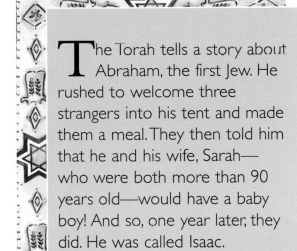

The Torah tells a story about Abraham, the first Jew. He rushed to welcome three strangers into his tent and made them a meal. They then told him that he and his wife, Sarah—who were both more than 90 years old—would have a baby boy! And so, one year later, they did. He was called Isaac.

A child puts coins in the family's tzedaka box.

"And when you reap the harvest of your land, you shall not reap all the way to the edges of your field . . . you shall leave them for the poor and the stranger."

(LEVITICUS 23: 22)

Daily Life and Worship

At home

More than anywhere else, home is the place where Judaism is practiced. It is where people pray every day, celebrate Shabbat every week, and take part in Jewish festivals every year. Most Jewish customs for the home are based on the teachings of the Torah. Parents are responsible for educating their children in the Jewish way of life.

Signs

A Jewish home is simply one in which Jewish people live. However, there are usually items that show that the home is Jewish. The most important is a small box on the doorpost. This contains a mezuzah, a little parchment handwritten with the words of the Shema (see page 21). The Shema is one of the most important Jewish prayers. It tells Jews that there is only one God. Seeing the mezuzah reminds Jews to obey God's commandments. Inside the house may be other things, such as Jewish books, especially prayer books and a copy of the Tenakh. Most people also own some ritual objects to help them observe Jewish festivals. These might be Shabbat candlesticks, or a Seder plate. The Seder plate is used to hold ritual foods for celebrating Pesach (see page 25).

The mezuzah is fixed to the doorpost on the right.

Prayer

Jews can pray to God anywhere and at any time. If they can't go to the synagogue, they can pray at home instead. Traditionally, Jewish men pray three times a day. When they pray, men wear a skullcap (a kippah), a prayer shawl (a tallit), and sometimes also tefillin (small boxes strapped to the head and arm which contain sentences from the Torah). They say the Shema prayer every morning and evening. Jews also bless God for their food before and after eating. Unlike men, Jewish women do not have to pray three times a day.

A boy prays wearing a kippah, tallit, and tefillin.

Friday evening

The beginning of the Shabbat on Friday evening is a special time. The mother lights the Shabbat candles, and the father blesses the children and thanks God for the wine and the bread. After the meal, the family might study part of the Torah together or sing Shabbat songs.

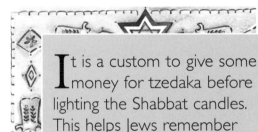

It is a custom to give some money for tzedaka before lighting the Shabbat candles. This helps Jews remember those who are less fortunate than themselves. After Shabbat has begun, money cannot be handled.

"Hear O Israel! The Lord is our God, the Lord alone. You shall love the Lord your God with all your heart and with all your soul and with all your might."

(THE BEGINNING OF THE SHEMA. DEUTERONOMY 6: 4–5).

At the synagogue

The synagogue is the Jewish house of prayer. Both men and women go there to pray as a community, although in a traditional synagogue the men and women sit separately. All synagogues hold services on Shabbat; some synagogues also hold services other days of the week. The weekday services are quite short, but the one on Shabbat morning lasts about two hours.

Inside the synagogue

On the synagogue wall that points towards Jerusalem, in Israel, is a cupboard or alcove called the ark. (In Europe and the United States, this will be on the eastern wall.) This cupboard contains the Torah scrolls. Everyone prays facing the ark. In front of the ark or in the middle of the room is a platform called the bimah, with a reading desk. It is from here that the Torah scroll is read aloud.

The eastern wall of a synagogue, showing the ark and the bimah.

Shabbat service

Every Shabbat morning in the synagogue, a section of the Torah is read aloud from the scroll. The sections follow in order, so each week in every synagogue the same part is being read. It is a great honor to be asked to read from the Torah. Before and after it is read, the scroll is carried in its mantle around the synagogue so everyone can see it.

Bar/Bat Mitzvah

On his 13th birthday, a boy becomes a Bar Mitzvah—a son of the commandments. He is now responsible for keeping God's commandments. He is also allowed to read from the Torah scroll at a service. He usually does this for the first time on the first Shabbat after his birthday. Practicing for this can take months, as it is very difficult. The ceremony is a happy occasion and is often followed by a party. A girl becomes a Bat Mitzvah—a daughter of the commandments—at 12 or 13. In a less traditional synagogue, she can read from the scroll in the same way that boys do, when she is 13.

"I make this covenant . . . not with you alone, but both with those who are standing here with us this day before the Lord our God and with those who are not with us here this day."

(DEUTERONOMY 29: 13-14)

Bar Mitzvahs are not mentioned in the Torah, although the idea of reaching religious adulthood at 13 is very old. The Bar Mitzvah ceremony started about 400 years ago in Germany. The first Bat Mitzvah took place in 1922, in the United States.

Two girls get ready for their Bat Mitzvah.

Torah festivals

The Jewish year is filled with festivals and special days. Some are happy and some are sad. Nearly all of them come from the Torah. Some festivals are based on things that Jews believe God asks them to do. Others remind Jews of stories in the Torah. Many festivals mark special times, such as the harvest, or important moments in Jewish history. Three festivals are especially connected with the Torah. They are Shavuot, Simchath Torah, and Pesach.

Flowers and greenery decorate the synagogue for Shavuot.

Shavuot

"Shavuot" means "weeks." On Shavuot, Jews remember how God gave Moses the Torah on Mount Sinai, seven weeks after the Israelites left Egypt. Some people stay up all night before Shavuot to study the Torah. This festival takes place in summer. It is celebrated by decorating the synagogue with greenery and eating milky foods, such as cheesecake.

Simchath Torah

It takes a whole year of Shabbat services to read through the Torah from one end to the other. The festival of Simchath Torah ("the Joy of the Torah") marks the end of that cycle, when the last chapter is read. But instead of waiting another week to start again, the beginning section is read right away. It is a special honor to be chosen to read either of these sections during the service. Simchath Torah is also celebrated with singing and dancing with the Torah scrolls.

Pesach

Pesach is also called Passover. It is the springtime festival that marks the escape of the children of Israel from slavery in Egypt. This is the biggest story in the whole of the Torah. Families celebrate it by holding a festive meal called a Seder, at which they retell the story. Several ritual foods are eaten, such as matzo (flat, unleavened bread). This is the only bread the Israelites had to eat when they left Egypt in a hurry.

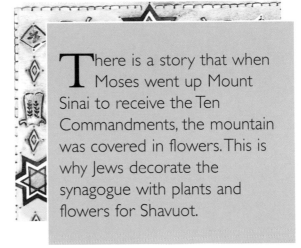

There is a story that when Moses went up Mount Sinai to receive the Ten Commandments, the mountain was covered in flowers. This is why Jews decorate the synagogue with plants and flowers for Shavuot.

A Jewish family holding a Seder together to celebrate Pesach.

"Surely, this Instruction which I enjoin upon you this day is not too baffling for you, nor is it beyond reach ... No, the thing is very close to you, in your mouth and in your heart, to observe it."

(DEUTERONOMY 30: 11–14)

Study and Reading

The importance of study

Education is one of the most important values in Judaism. It is even more important for a Jewish community to build a Torah school than a synagogue. Jewish children need to learn to read Hebrew, because it is the language of the Torah and of the prayers. It is also a language that Jews all around the world have in common and often use for communicating with each other. But education is not just for children. Jews are supposed to carry on studying the Torah throughout their lives.

Children

All Jewish parents are responsible for educating their children. Some of this education happens at home. However, most synagogues run a religion school as well. It is open on Sunday mornings and sometimes after school during the week. Children discuss the Torah, learn Hebrew, and study the Jewish way of life. They can start religion school as young as three years old and leave when they have become Bar or Bat Mitzvah. Some children stay until they are 16.

When they are worn out, old Torah scrolls are buried in a Jewish cemetery or stored away. This is because they contain the name of God and are holy. In fact, anything with God's name on it cannot be destroyed—including old prayerbooks and even photocopies.

"Moses summoned all the Israelites and said to them, 'Hear, O Israel, the laws and rules that I proclaim to you this day! Study them and observe them faithfully!'" (DEUTERONOMY 5: 1)

Jews studying the Torah in a yeshiva in Jerusalem, Israel.

Adults

After leaving school, some young people spend a year studying Judaism in a yeshiva (Jewish college). Here they study the Torah and other Jewish books. They often work with a friend, discussing what the teachings really mean. Adults can continue learning about Judaism by going to classes at their synagogue. They might also read at home—perhaps with a study partner. It is customary to read through the week's Torah section before hearing it at the synagogue on Shabbat.

Respect for the Torah

When people study the Torah, they do not usually use a scroll. They read from the Five Books of Moses printed as a book. But, like the Torah scroll, the book is treated with respect. Holy books are not scribbled in, banged on the table, or put on the floor. No other books can be put on top of the Torah. Men and boys usually wear a kippah when studying the Torah, to show respect for God and His teachings.

Glossary

Abraham The first Jew; the first person to believe in one God.

Ark The cupboard or alcove in a synagogue in which the Torah scrolls are kept.

Ark of the covenant The special chest in which the children of Israel carried the tablets of the Ten Commandments through the desert.

Bar Mitzvah "Son of the Commandments." Also the name for the ceremony at which a boy becomes, in religious terms, an adult.

Bat Mitzvah "Daughter of the Commandments." Also the name for the ceremony at which a girl becomes, in religious terms, an adult.

Bimah The raised platform at the front or in the middle of a synagogue. The Torah is read from a desk which stands on this platform.

Canaan The name in the Torah for the country that is Israel today. Also known as the "Promised Land."

Children of Israel The descendants of Abraham's grandson, Jacob (whose name was later changed to Israel). This is another name for the Jewish people.

Covenant An agreement made between the children of Israel and God, describing their special relationship.

Golden Rule A rule, held across many religions, that tells people to treat others as they would like to be treated themselves.

Halakhah "The way on which one goes." The set of Jewish laws that guides religious Jews through everyday life.

Hebrew The language of the Torah and of Jewish prayer. Spoken in daily life in Israel and as a second language by many Jews in other countries.

Holocaust / Shoah The murder of six million Jews by Nazi Germany during World War II (1939-1945).

Idol A statue or picture that is worshipped as a god.

Israel A name for the Jewish people. It also refers to the State of Israel, founded in 1948.

Judah The fourth son of Jacob, and leader of one of the 12 Tribes of Israel.

Kippah A type of cap worn by Jewish men (and occasionally women) for prayer and religious study.

Kosher A word which is usually used to describe food which Jews are allowed to eat.

Mantle The cover, often velvet, with which the Torah scroll is "dressed" when it is not being read.

Matzo The flat, unleavened bread that is eaten at Pesach.

Mezuzah (plural, **mezuzot**) A little square of parchment with the Shema prayer written on it. It is placed in a container and fixed on the doorpost of Jewish homes.

Moses / Moshe Rabbenu "Moses Our Teacher." The great Jewish leader who led the children of Israel out of slavery in Egypt and to whom God gave the Torah.

Pesach The festival of Passover, which celebrates the escape of the children of Israel from slavery in Egypt.

Promised Land Another name for the Land of Canaan. The land promised by God in the Torah to Abraham and his descendants.

Prophets People who received messages from God and spoke to others about them. The second part of the Tenakh is also known as The Prophets because each book in it is named after one of them.

Rabbi A respected Jewish teacher and community leader.

Seder The ritual family meal during which the story of the Jews' escape from slavery is told. It is held in the home on the first two evenings of Pesach.

Shabbat The seventh and holiest day of the week, which falls on Saturday for Jews. This is a rest day, and no work is done.

Shavuot The festival in summer that marks the time when the Jews received God's Torah from Moses on Mount Sinai.

Shema One of the most important prayers, said daily. It says that there is only one God, and asks Jews to remember this always. It is found inside mezuzot and tefillin.

Simchath Torah The festival in autumn celebrating the end of one cycle of reading through the Torah during Shabbat services, and the immediate beginning of the next.

Sofer The person who writes Torah scrolls and the parchments for mezuzot and tefillin, by hand.

Synagogue A Jewish house of prayer. Services are held here weekly and sometimes daily, as well as community events and classes for children and adults.

Tallit The prayer shawl worn by men and sometimes, in less traditional synagogues, women. Each corner has a tassel knotted in a certain way to represent the name of God.

Tefillin Small black boxes containing the Shema prayer. One is strapped to the forehead and another to the upper arm before praying.

Tenakh The book of Jewish sacred texts, consisting of the Torah, the Prophets, and the Writings. The name comes from the first letter of the names of these three books in Hebrew (Torah, Nevi'im, Ketuvim).

Ten Commandments The 10 laws that God wrote down on tablets of stone for Moses to give to the children of Israel.

Tikkun Olam "The repair of the world." Jews see their role as helping to make the world a better place.

Torah / The Five Books of Moses The first five books, and the most sacred part, of the Tenakh. Together they are called the Torah, and are read from a scroll.

Tzedaka "Doing righteous acts." Includes giving money to those who need it.

Writings The third part of the Tenakh. It includes poetry, stories, and proverbs.

Yeshiva A college where some young Jewish men go to study Jewish texts such as the Torah.

Index

John Besh

Jose Andres

Jason Cunningham

Eric Ripert

Terrance Brennan

Matthew Kenney

Gabriel Kreuther

Phil Evans

Erik Blauberg

Dan Barber

Thomas Keller

Charlie Trotter

Todd English